The author
In 1981 Didier Boursin obtained a diploma
in Architecture (DPLG) from the École
Nationale Supérieure des Beaux-Arts. A
teacher of fine art, architecture, and design,
he received the architectural prize, Villa
Médicis, in 1984, and in 1986 he opened a
fashion boutique in Paris with Setsuko.

He is the chief editor of the review *Le Pli*
and has been the president of an association
of 'paper folding' for the past five years. He
contributes as a 'folding expert' to a number
of French publications and takes part in
many shows devoted to this craft. Today,
there is a great demand for his diverse
creations (aesthetic, playful, functional,
etc.), all based upon folding.

For my parents

Creative Napkin Folding

DIDIER BOURSIN

SEARCH PRESS

First published in Great Britain 1993
Search Press Limited,
Wellwood, North Farm Road,
Tunbridge Wells, Kent TN2 3DR

English translation copyright © Search Press Limited 1993

Originally published in France by Dessain et Tolra, Paris
Copyright © Dessain et Tolra 1991

Translated by Giles de la Bédoyère

The author would like to thank the following people for their help in the making of this book: for research, François Dulac in France, Roberto Morassi in Italy, Paula Mulatinho in Germany, and Vincente Palacios in Spain; Daniel Morcrette of Luzarches for his advice and the loan of illustrations for the Introduction; Setsuko for his advice; Yoshihide Momotani of Japan for the Rose-bud design; David Brill for the 'Da Sisto' man; the company Le Jacquard Française for supplying the pure cotton damask napkins used in this book; and Établissements Sagnet and Madame Besse for the loan of accessories. Finally, he would like to thank Kayoko Weiss for styling and Fabrice Besse the talented photographer.

Layout: Michèle Andrault   Design: Graphic Hainaut
Photogravure: Atelier Fossard

ISBN 0 85532 760 X (Hb)
ISBN 0 85532 750 2 (Pb)

Printed in Spain by A. G. Elkar, S. Coop. 48012 Bilbao

Contents

Introduction

1. Double-headed eagle. 2. Dog.
3. Lion. 4. Dolphin. 5. Tortoise.
6. Bear. 7. Pelican. 8. Small bird.
9. Hare. 10. Crab. 11. Chicken.
12. Capons. 13. Bird on a tower.
14. Cock on the hen. 15. Peacock.
16. Lion of St Mark.

Engraving taken from the treatise on the folding of napkins, Li Tre Trattati (The Three Treatises), *by Mattia Giegher, published in Padua in 1639 by Paolo Frambotto.*
Coll. D. Morcrette.

The history of the napkin is connected with that of the tablecloth, and it goes back as far as the Romans, who used napkins to wipe their faces. These were almost always white and sometimes bordered with gold thread. All guests were expected to bring their own and look after them as napkins were rare and much sought after!

Between Roman and medieval times the history of the napkin is lost due to lack of evidence. It is regained in the Middle Ages, when neither cloths nor plates were used. Instead, trenches were carved into the table surface, taking the place of plates. However, cloths were used on special occasions – some so large (as much as twelve metres by four) that they had to be folded. The historian 'Le Grand d'Aussy', nineteenth century author of *Histoire de la vie privée des Français* (*History of French Domestic Life*), tells us, 'Such enormous widths of cloth for refectory tables required folding for practical use'. As time went on, it became the practice to pile up any number from two to five cloths as the meal's courses progressed. Wooden plates and fingers were employed for eating, along with a single knife, and hands and mouths were wiped on the cloth itself! In about the thirteenth century, the roller-towel appeared. This was a long piece of cloth used for wiping the hands, which was attached by a stick to the wall.

It was not until the sixteenth century that the napkin proper entered the gastronomic stage. In 1530, Erasmus wrote in his work on etiquette that 'the napkin must be borne on the left shoulder and used to wipe the mouth before drinking'. In an engraving by Abraham Bosse you can see a woman, not a servant, seated with a napkin on her left arm. The first writings on napkin folding date from 1560. In Venice, Domenico Romoli published a summary entitled the *Singolare Dottrina*, in which he described both napkin and tablecloth folding with admirable precision. In sixteenth century France, Henri III (as reported by Le Grand d'Aussy) 'desired that his tablecloths be folded with great art, like the ruffs worn about the throat'. According to Arthur Thomas, 'Such folding strongly resembled an undulating river whose surface a gentle breeze disturbed'. In 1600, at the wedding of Marie de Médicis and Henri IV in Florence, the table of honour was composed of 'foldings and pastries'. The napkins were folded in different ways and, being of white Rheims linen, represented a winter hunting scene.

A few years later, napkin folding acquired its first theoretician, Mattia Giegher, a German, who published *Li Tre Trattati* (*The Three Treatises*) in Padua in 1639, which included a series of remarkable engravings of napkin and linen tablecloth folding. Firstly, they demonstrated the position of the hands and the required folding movements, then they showed the elaborate finished pieces. These were all animal shapes, with waxen or wooden heads attached. Certain details, such as crabs' claws, were made from bread dough. Sometimes sewing was used to keep the shapes, and bread rolls were placed underneath to provide volume.

In 1665, Georg Philipp Harsdörfer published the *Völlstandiges Vermehrtes Trincir-Buch* in Nuremberg, which reproduced Giegher's engravings. He emphasized that these 'foldings' should be used for banquets and feasts, and that they were purely decorative and temporary embellishments. The most beautiful creations were for exalted guests, the less distinguished creations sufficing for the lower end of the table. Harsdörfer suggested that they might invite reflection and promote conversation. These 'feasts for the eye' often had a hidden symbolic meaning. A dog signified fidelity, a peacock immortality. A triumphal arch, pyramids, and even a palace were designed to mark a peace banquet – all in folded cloth! They had an undeniable beauty. In the same book, Harsdörfer also printed simpler foldings, such as an abbot's cowl, a clown's cap, and a lily – designs resembling modern napkin folding.

In 1692, L'Ecuyer-Tranchant de la Varenne published a cookery book, *Le Vrai Cuisinier François* (*The Authentic French Chef*), in which he explained the rudiments of napkin folding: 'Firstly, one must know how to mould and crimp, these being the skills most necessary for the practice of this delicate art'. Moulding refers to intricate folding, and crimping signifies folding into accordion shapes. The technique is simple and with it you can achieve a great variety of shapes, such as double shells, melon, hen, partridge, pheasant, hare, rabbit, tortoise, and Cross of Lorraine. Giles Rose, Maître d'hôtel to Charles II of England, produced an instruction manual for officials of 'La Bouche', in which there were similar patterns to those in *The Authentic French Chef*. In 1701, Glorez published a résumé illustrated by superb engravings of napkin folding, completing the splendid literature written on this theme.

In the sixteenth century, the napkin, square or rectangular, was often as large as a metre square, and it was tied beneath the chin to protect the shirt-front. At the start of the twentieth century it was reduced in size to a small, square piece of cloth and was decorated in increasingly varied ways. Today, the elaborate effects of the past have also been replaced by much simpler designs which require less preparation.

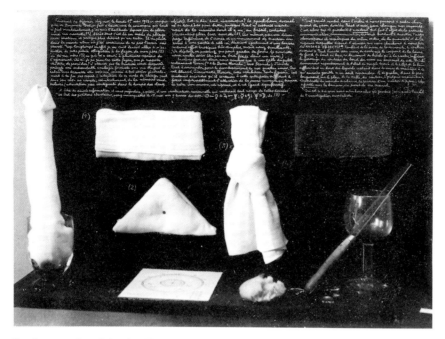

In the words of André Breton:

Finishing breakfast at my house on Monday 1 May 1933 with Benjamin Péret, I remarked aloud that recently I had adopted an automatic habit of folding my napkin in such and such a way (1). It was, after all, a practical method of doing so, and less 'showy' than most. Also, I was content that it was my own way; for too long had I adopted the method taught to me by my parents – my father's (2), or my mother's (3) – a fact which used to exasperate me. Where, I wondered, had I learned this technique, whose appearance so closely resembled the shape of my tobacco-pouch (4), frequently laid beside the napkin after a meal? Perhaps it could be attributed to the association by sight of the two neighbouring articles . . . Was that all, however? Was there not a hint of sexual symbolism? Péret told me how he had seen diners in Brazil fold their napkins in the shape of half-peeled bananas (5) – a disturbingly erotic effect! (Incidentally, I regret the fact that, to ensure stability, I have to stick the rolled napkin into a glass.)

The same day, at dinner, we were six at a table in a small restaurant ('A La Dame Blanche'). I requested Péret to re-create the 'napkin parade' for the diversion of our fellow diners: Crevel, Éluard, Giacometti, Thirion. His momentary absorption attracted the attention of the young waitress as she crossed the room and her smile, speedily suppressed, was suggestive. When we had returned to normal, she passed behind Péret and myself to replace our cutlery. It was then that the *accident* occurred which I wish to describe here, in hope of provoking observations whose weight and diversity may influence opinion on the question of 'objective risk'.*

The knife intended for Péret, falling from the waitress's hand, struck the drinking-glass, splitting it downwards and leaving only the base intact. The split, however, remained a mere crack in the glass, did not spill any of the wine, and pleased Péret by its aesthetic effect against the liquid's warm glow. Let me add that this effect was enhanced by the presence of a bread roll (not far from the fallen knife-blade) having the sexual implication earlier attributed to the banana.

And, finally, though I append this without prejudice or any wish to rule out a rational explanation, may I remind the reader of a remarkable disposition of the planets on 1 May about 9.00 p.m [illegible] (7).

*Confirming more than ever the significance of our exploration of surrealism.

This book contains over forty napkin folding projects, some traditional and some newly created. They are arranged according to their degree of difficulty, from the very simple to the advanced, and each one is explained with clear, step-by-step diagrams. Some are more suitable for decorating a table centre than individual place-settings, as their complexity makes their duplication rather impractical, e.g. the Hedgehog (see pages 90–1). Others have been designed especially to hold warmed rolls, toast, or even a present, e.g. the Cushion (see pages 36–7), and the Gift-wrapper (see pages 56–7).

Of the models in this book, I have created the Shirt, Cutlery holder, House, Waves, Fish, Flamenco, Pleating, Ear of corn, Orchid, and Shepherd designs. I hope that they will inspire many others from my readers – the more the merrier.

Materials and techniques

Apart from clean hands and a good working space, all you need to create the napkin designs shown in this book is a square piece of fabric. Linen, cotton, or synthetic fabrics, in embroidered or printed damask, are all suitable, so long as their texture and colour are right for the effect required. You will need to starch the material first, in order to give it sufficient stiffness, and ironing is also recommended for complex pleating and less amenable fabrics.

Before attempting any of the projects, it is a good idea to check the diagrams below and practise the techniques on a piece of paper. Mastery of these basic folds, together with a knowledge of the key, will help you to achieve perfect results.

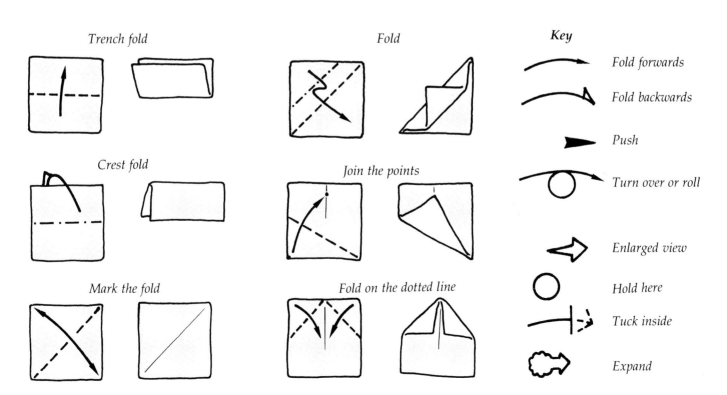

Trench fold	Fold	Key
Crest fold	Join the points	Fold forwards / Fold backwards / Push / Turn over or roll / Enlarged view / Hold here / Tuck inside / Expand
Mark the fold	Fold on the dotted line	

Square

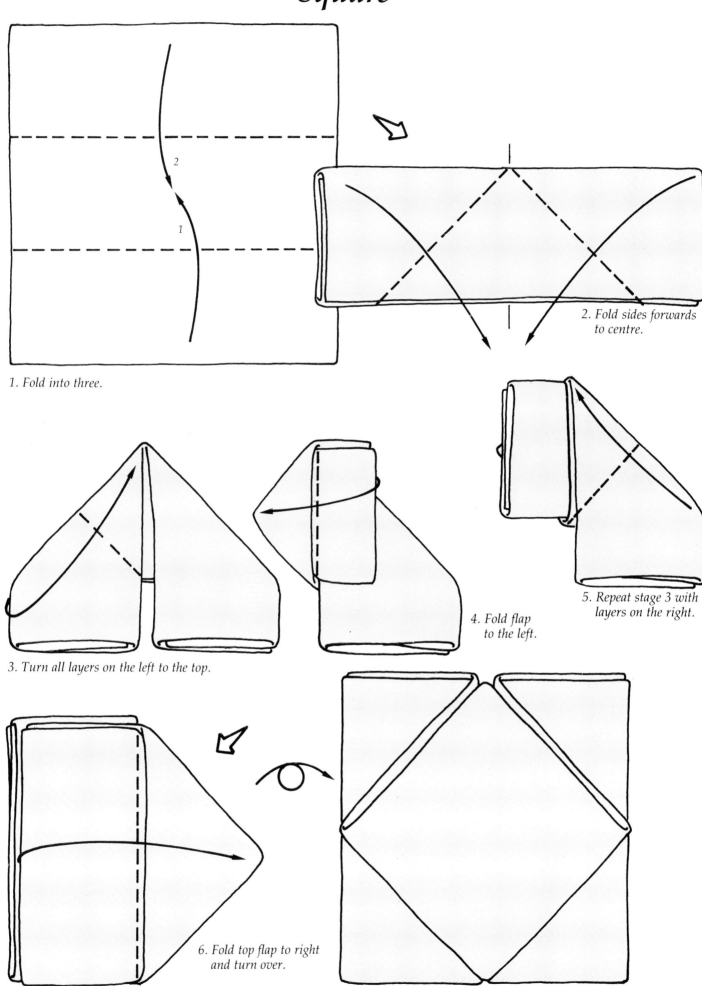

1. Fold into three.

2. Fold sides forwards to centre.

3. Turn all layers on the left to the top.

4. Fold flap to the left.

5. Repeat stage 3 with layers on the right.

6. Fold top flap to right and turn over.

Shirt

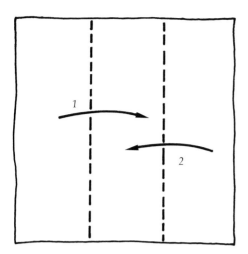

1. Fold into three.

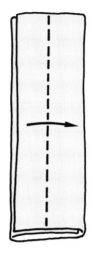

2. Fold one side in half.

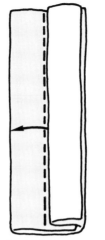

3. Fold the underneath side in half.

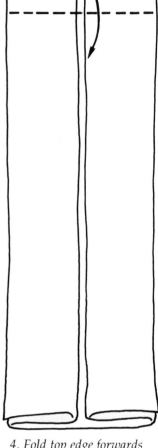

4. Fold top edge forwards and turn over.

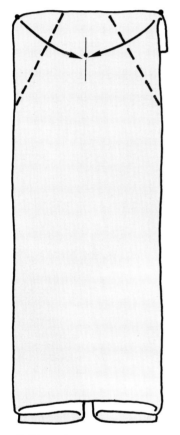

5. Turn down corners to centre front.

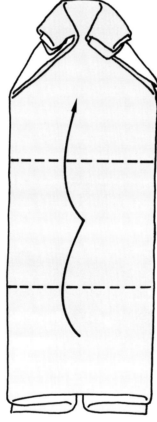

6. Fold into three from bottom upwards and tuck folded edge under collar.

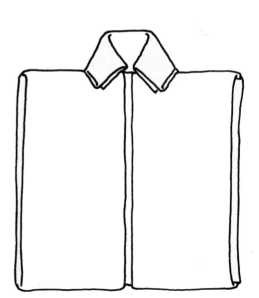

Tea-time

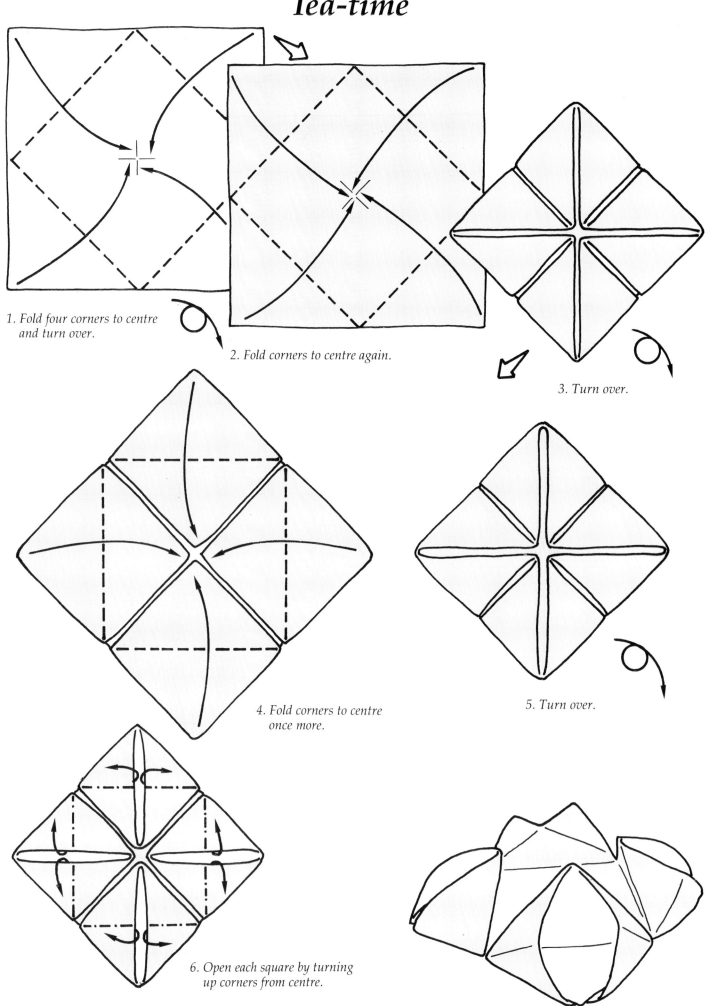

1. Fold four corners to centre and turn over.

2. Fold corners to centre again.

3. Turn over.

4. Fold corners to centre once more.

5. Turn over.

6. Open each square by turning up corners from centre.

Cutlery holder

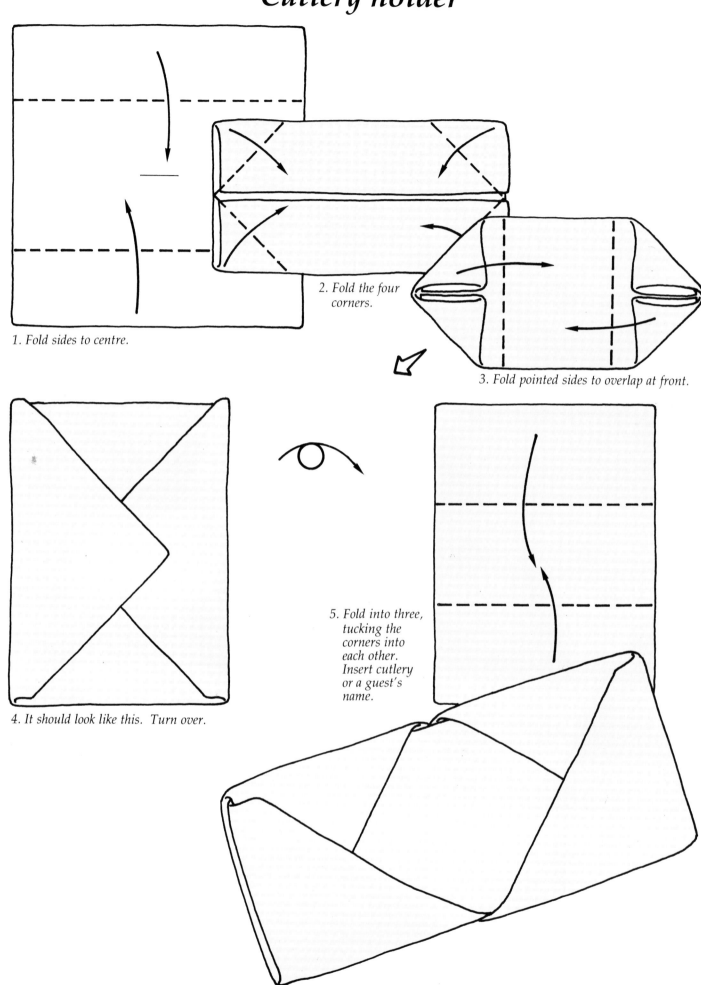

1. Fold sides to centre.

2. Fold the four corners.

3. Fold pointed sides to overlap at front.

4. It should look like this. Turn over.

5. Fold into three, tucking the corners into each other. Insert cutlery or a guest's name.

Shirt-front

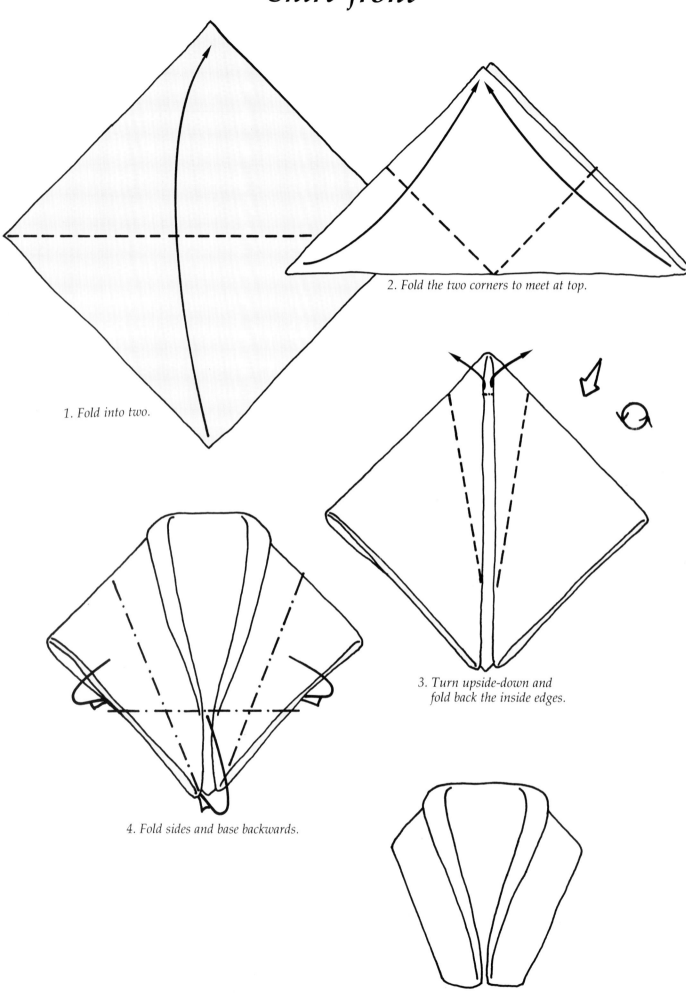

1. Fold into two.

2. Fold the two corners to meet at top.

3. Turn upside-down and fold back the inside edges.

4. Fold sides and base backwards.

Napkin-ring

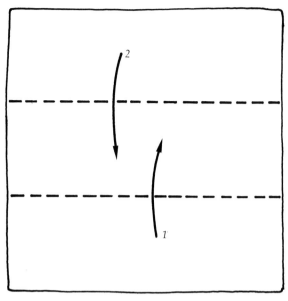

1. Fold into three.

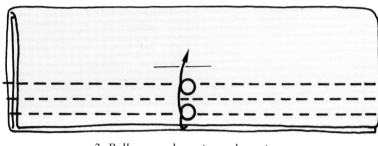

2. Roll up one layer towards centre.

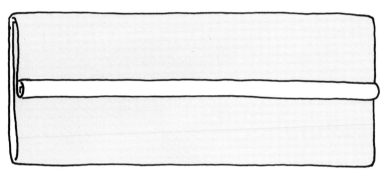

3. It should look like this. Turn over.

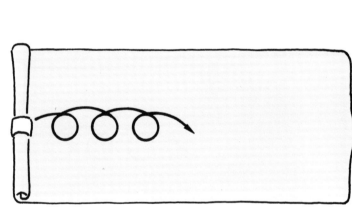

4. Roll the strip tightly from one end to the other.

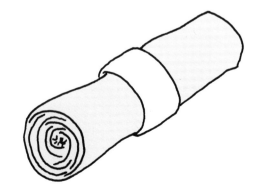

Cocoon

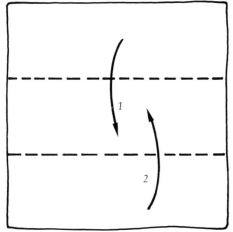

1. Fold into three.

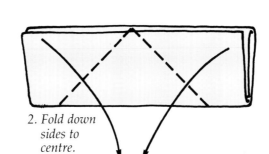

2. Fold down sides to centre.

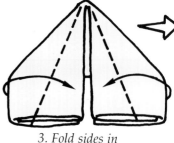

3. Fold sides in half to centre.

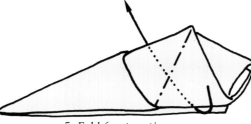

5. Fold front section back to inside.

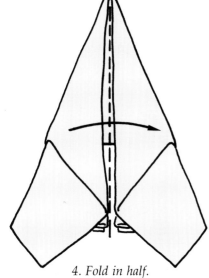

4. Fold in half.

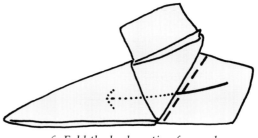

6. Fold the back section forwards and tuck inside.

7. Pull down four front flaps as shown, then fold tallest flap to side and back.

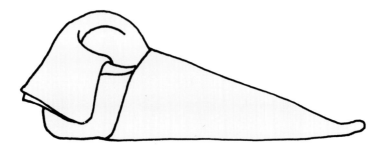

Fleur-de-lis

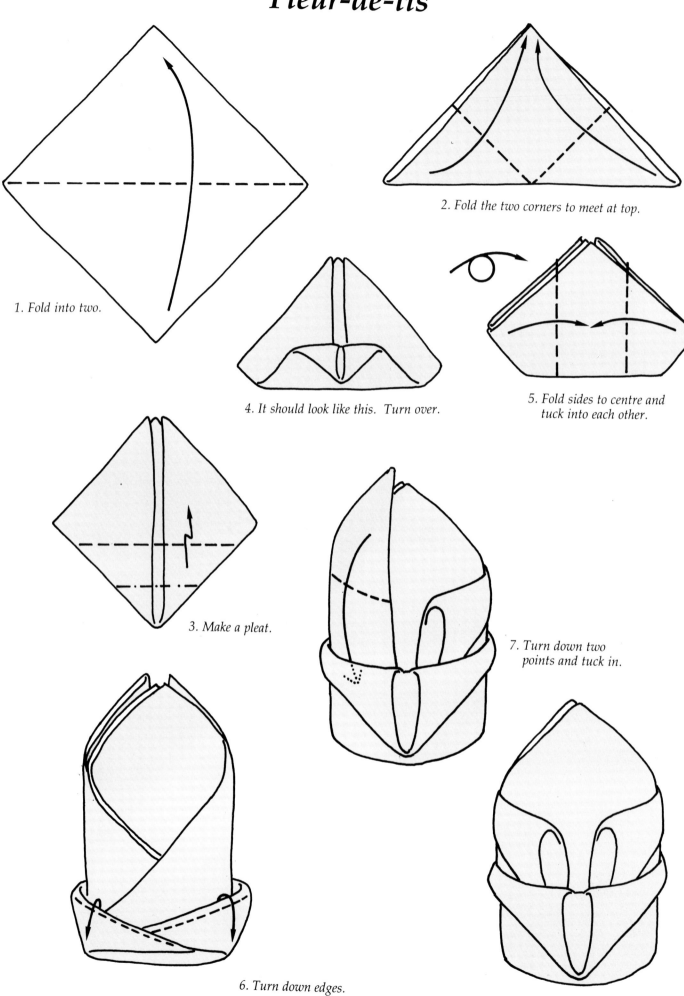

1. Fold into two.

2. Fold the two corners to meet at top.

3. Make a pleat.

4. It should look like this. Turn over.

5. Fold sides to centre and tuck into each other.

6. Turn down edges.

7. Turn down two points and tuck in.

Hare

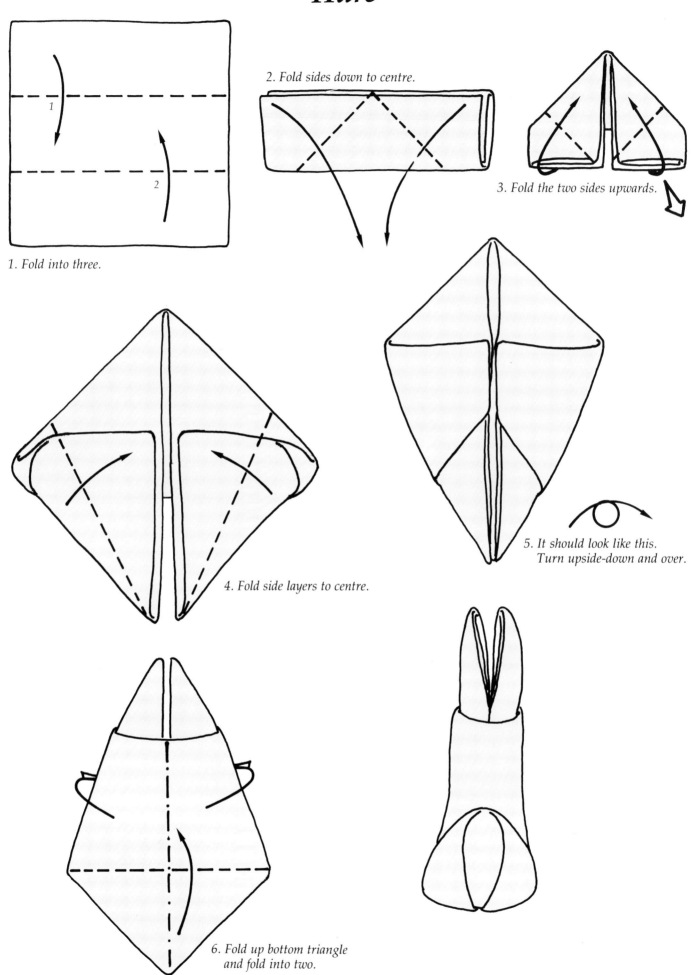

1. Fold into three.

2. Fold sides down to centre.

3. Fold the two sides upwards.

4. Fold side layers to centre.

5. It should look like this.
Turn upside-down and over.

6. Fold up bottom triangle
and fold into two.

Bird of paradise

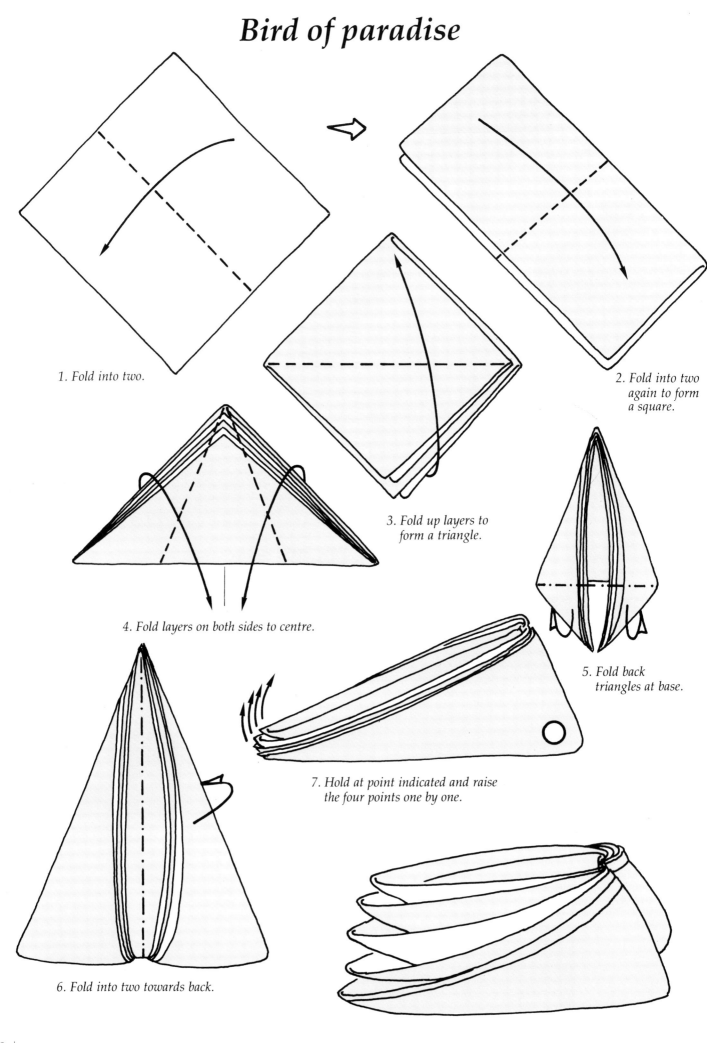

1. Fold into two.

2. Fold into two again to form a square.

3. Fold up layers to form a triangle.

4. Fold layers on both sides to centre.

5. Fold back triangles at base.

6. Fold into two towards back.

7. Hold at point indicated and raise the four points one by one.

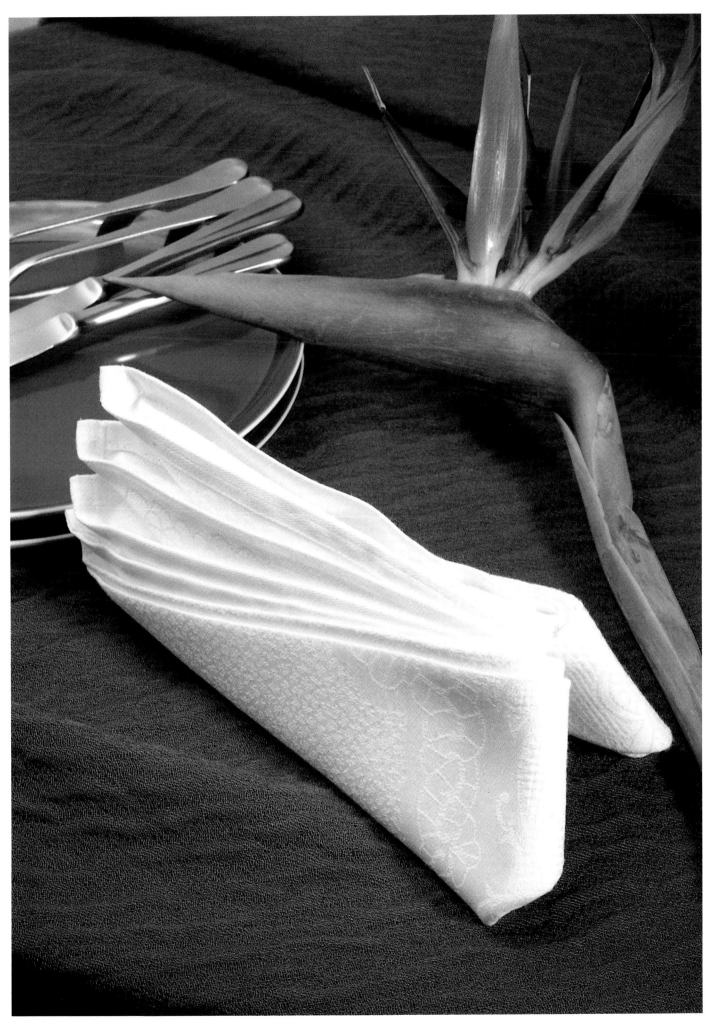

Mitre

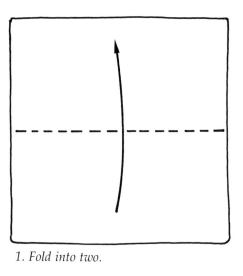

1. Fold into two.

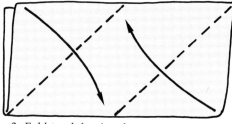

2. Fold top left triangle to centre and bottom right to centre.

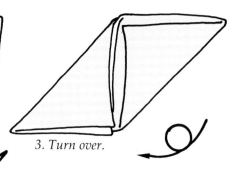

3. Turn over.

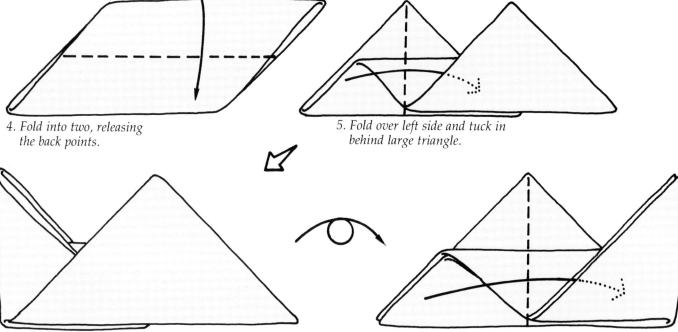

4. Fold into two, releasing the back points.

5. Fold over left side and tuck in behind large triangle.

6. It should look like this. Turn over.

7. Repeat stage 5.

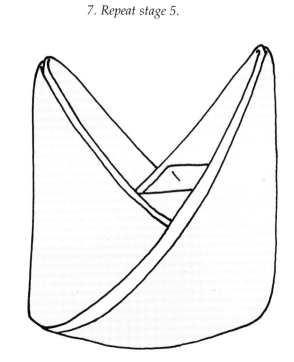

8. Open out.

House

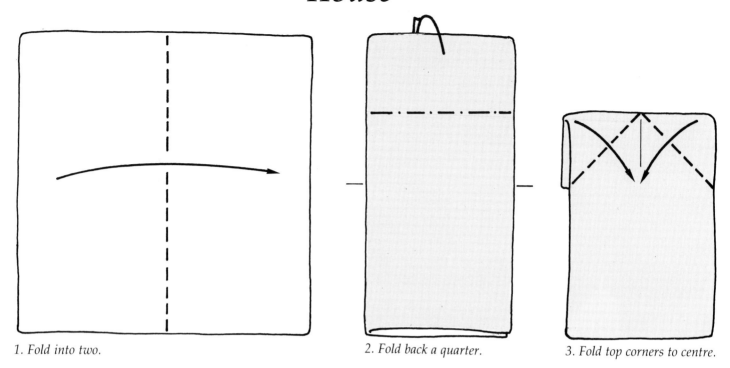

1. Fold into two.

2. Fold back a quarter.

3. Fold top corners to centre.

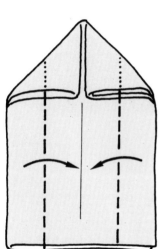

4. Fold sides to centre, tucking top corners under triangles. Turn over.

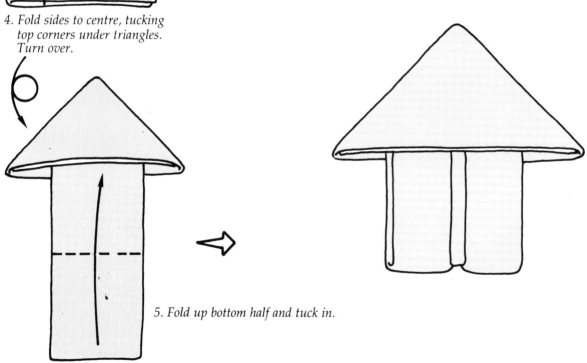

5. Fold up bottom half and tuck in.

Purse

1. Fold corners to centre.

2. Fold in half towards top.

3. Fold into three.

4. Open top triangle and take point to centre.

5. Fold down top and tuck in.

Cushion

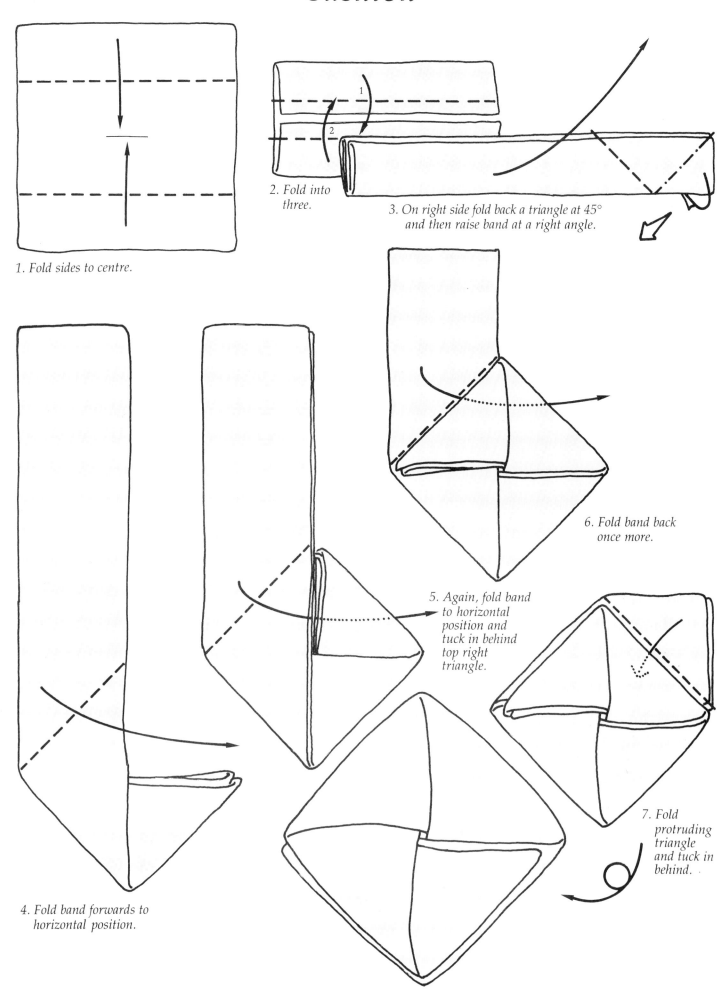

1. Fold sides to centre.

2. Fold into three.

3. On right side fold back a triangle at 45° and then raise band at a right angle.

4. Fold band forwards to horizontal position.

5. Again, fold band to horizontal position and tuck in behind top right triangle.

6. Fold band back once more.

7. Fold protruding triangle and tuck in behind.

Boatlets

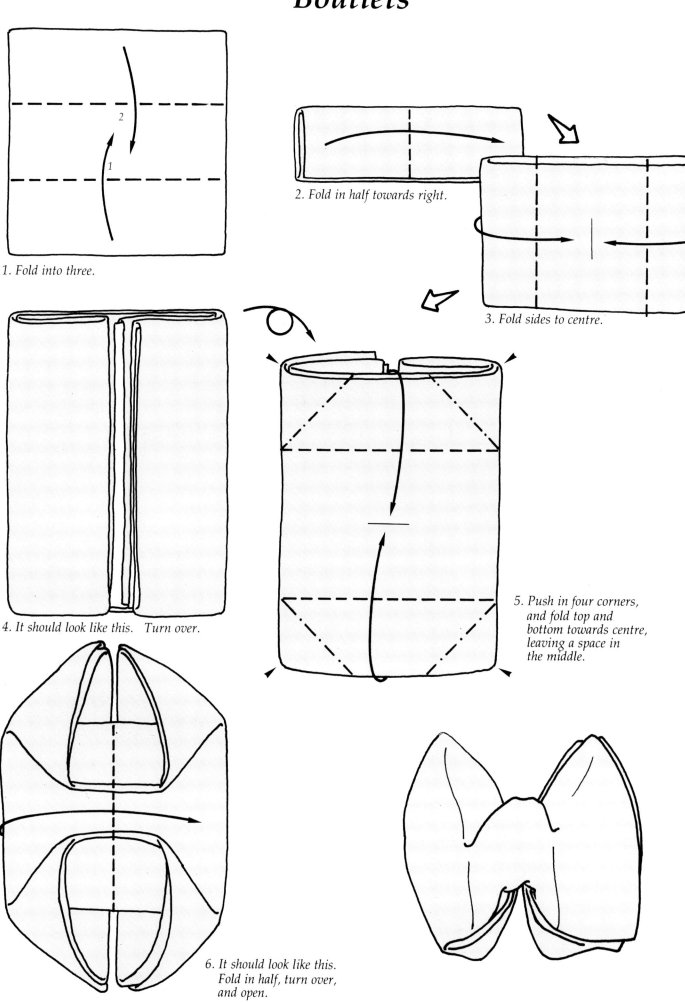

1. Fold into three.

2. Fold in half towards right.

3. Fold sides to centre.

4. It should look like this. Turn over.

5. Push in four corners, and fold top and bottom towards centre, leaving a space in the middle.

6. It should look like this. Fold in half, turn over, and open.

Candle

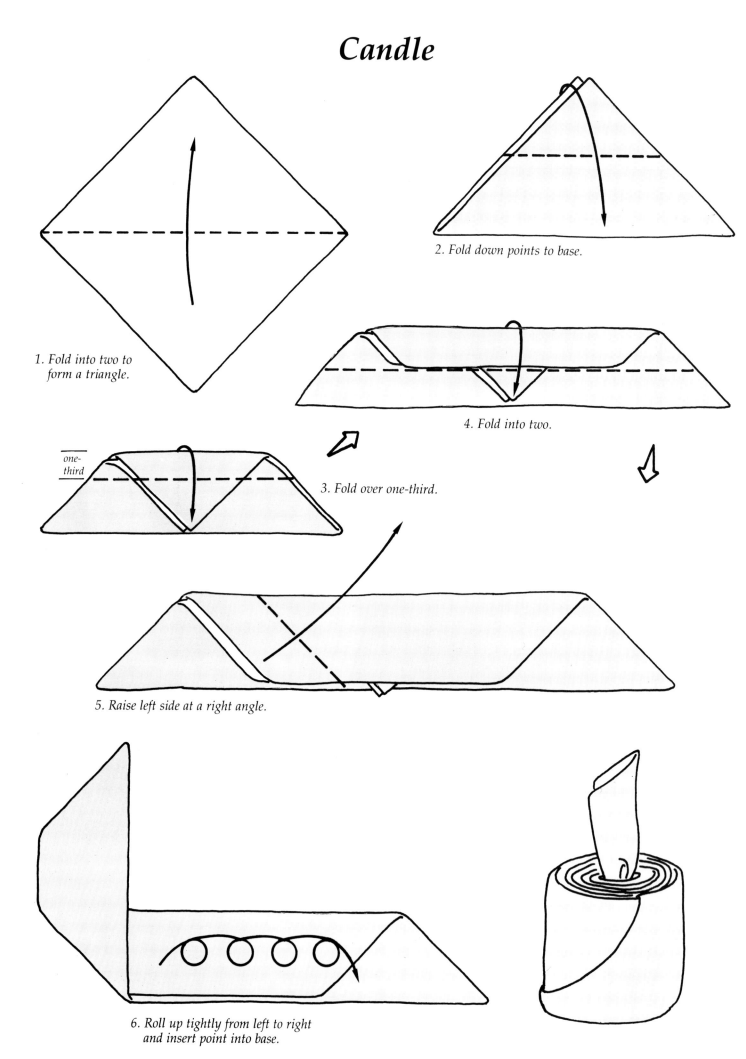

1. Fold into two to form a triangle.

2. Fold down points to base.

3. Fold over one-third.

one-third

4. Fold into two.

5. Raise left side at a right angle.

6. Roll up tightly from left to right and insert point into base.

Rabbit

1. Fold in half to form a triangle.

2. Fold sides one over the other.

3. Fold the two triangles to centre.

4. Fold down top.

5. Fold sides back, tucking them into each other. Turn over.

6. Fold into two and tuck triangle into top.

7. Turn round and press out sides.

Cicada

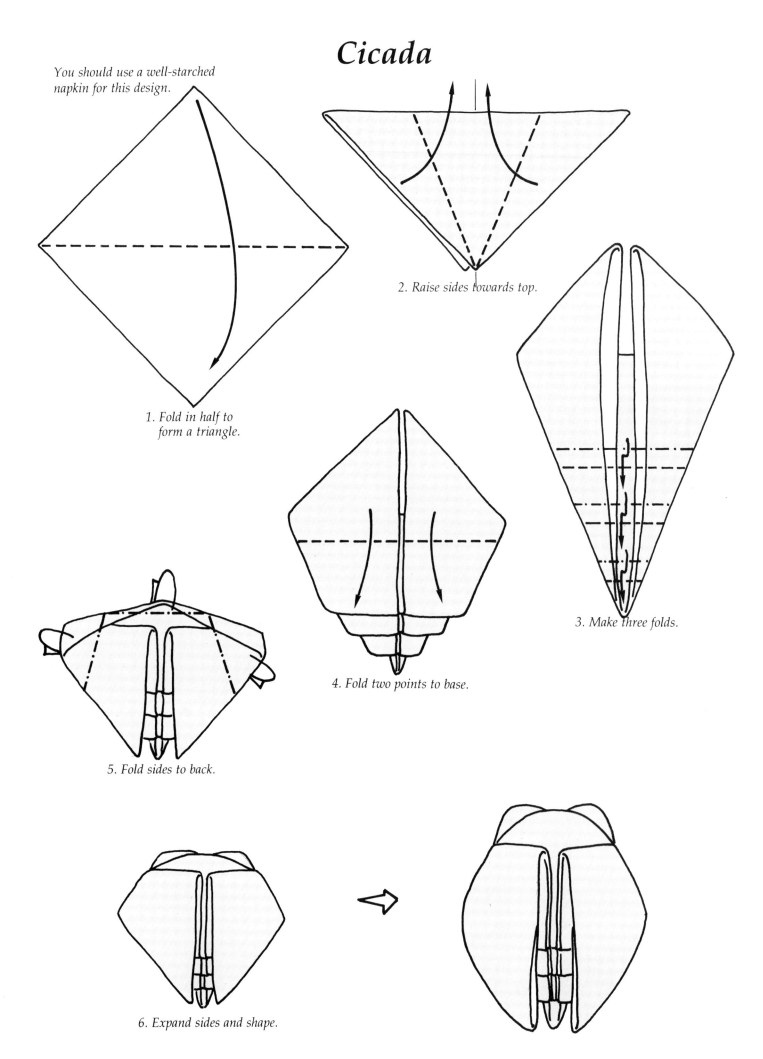

You should use a well-starched napkin for this design.

1. Fold in half to form a triangle.

2. Raise sides towards top.

3. Make three folds.

4. Fold two points to base.

5. Fold sides to back.

6. Expand sides and shape.

Cone

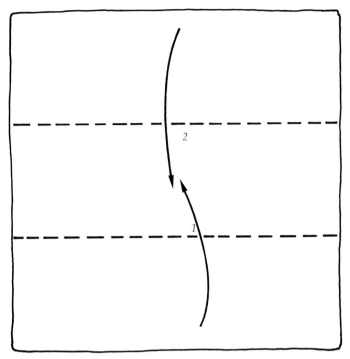

1. Fold into three.

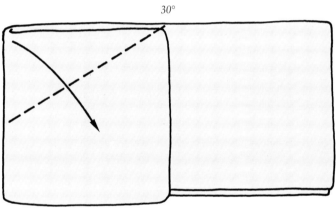

2. Fold one-third to the right.

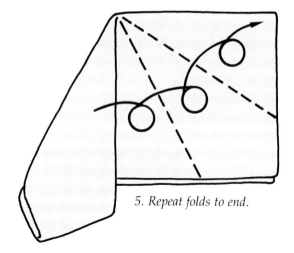

3. Fold down top corner at 30°.

4. Fold down again to a right angle.

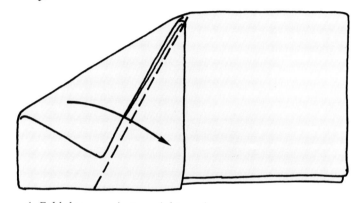

5. Repeat folds to end.

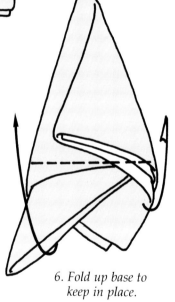

6. Fold up base to keep in place.

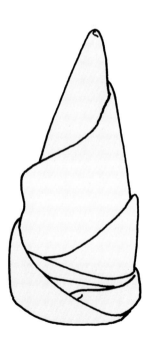

Bud

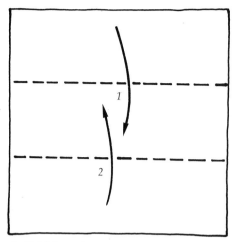

1. Fold into three.

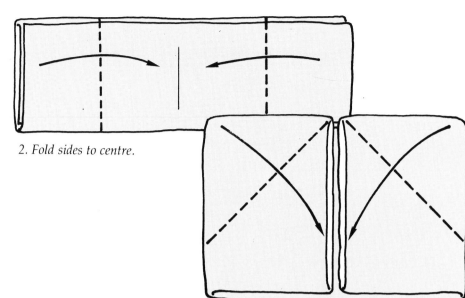

2. Fold sides to centre.

3. Fold top corners to centre.

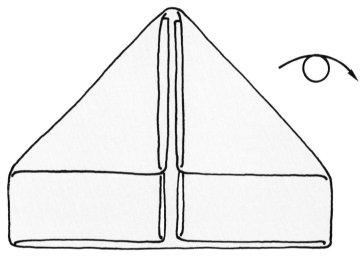

4. It should look like this.
   Turn upside-down and over.

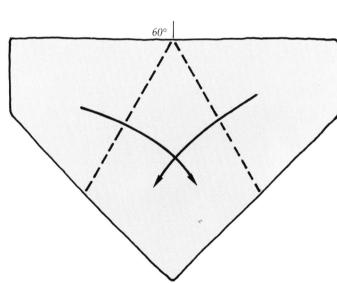

5. Fold into three and tuck in corners.

6. It should look like this.
   Turn over and expand.

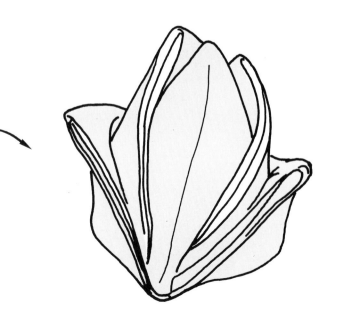

Crown

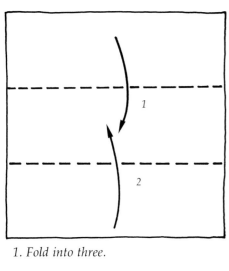

1. Fold into three.

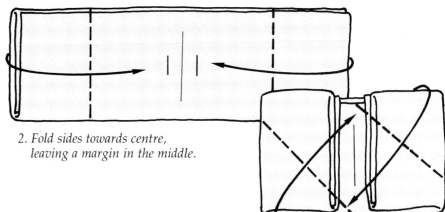

2. Fold sides towards centre, leaving a margin in the middle.

3. Fold opposite triangles to centre.

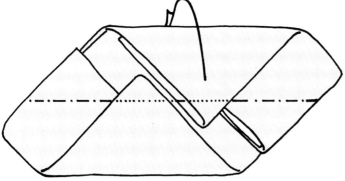

4. Fold in half to back releasing points.

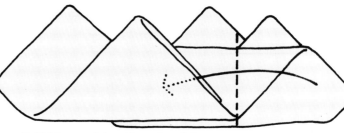

5. Fold over right side and tuck in.

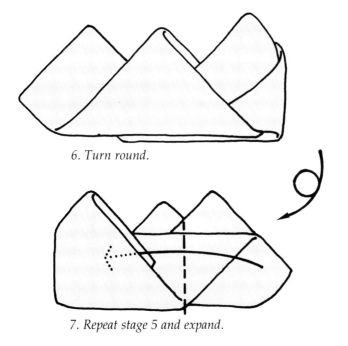

6. Turn round.

7. Repeat stage 5 and expand.

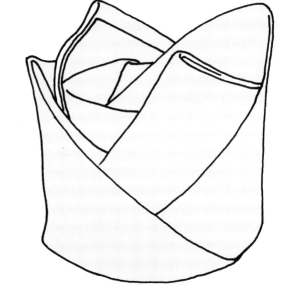

Waves

1. Fold into two.

2. Fold into two again from left to right.

3. Turn clockwise and fold up top layer to point marked.

4. Repeat with second layer.

5. Repeat again with third layer.

6. Finally, repeat with fourth layer.

7. From centre, fold back sides.

8. Fold back rear triangle as shown and fold in half.

'Da Sisto' man

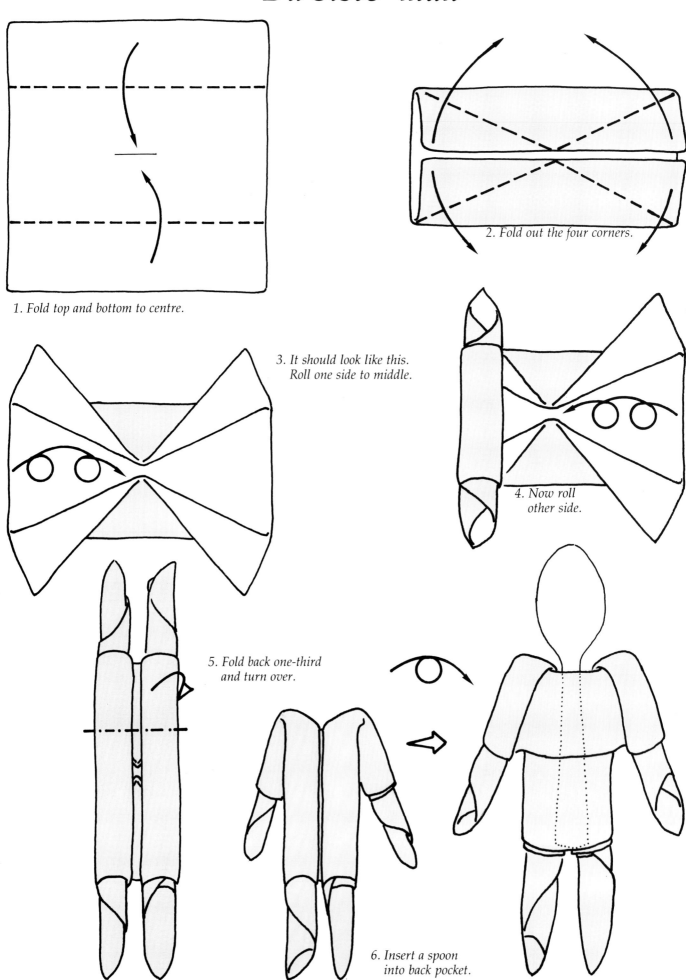

1. Fold top and bottom to centre.

2. Fold out the four corners.

3. It should look like this.
Roll one side to middle.

4. Now roll other side.

5. Fold back one-third and turn over.

6. Insert a spoon into back pocket.

Gift-wrapper

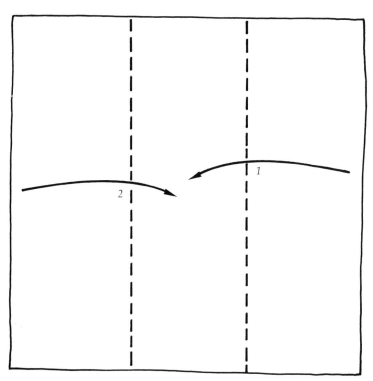

1. Fold into three.

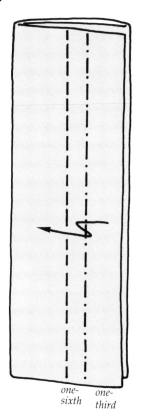

one-
sixth   one-
third

2. Make a pleat
   in top flap to
   proportions
   shown.

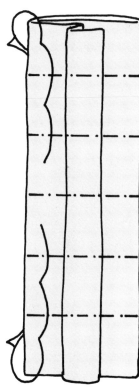

3. Fold back top
   and bottom,
   each into
   three equal
   parts.

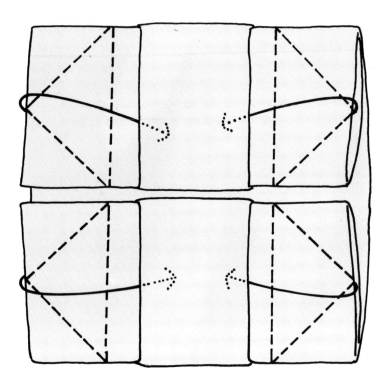

4. Open each part and slide point under
   central band. Place gift in the middle.

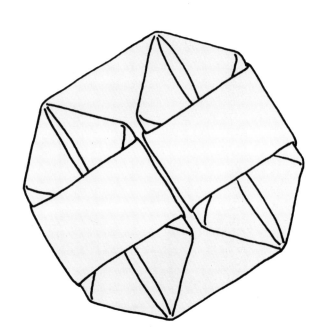

Triangle

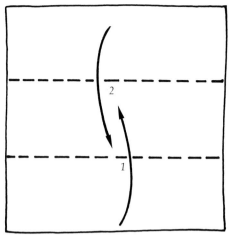

1. Fold into three.

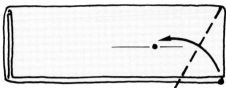

2. Fold bottom right corner to point indicated.

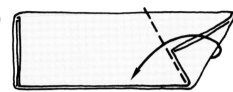

3. Fold again from right to left.

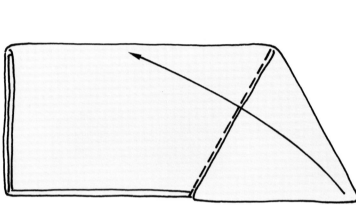

4. Fold bottom triangle to top edge.

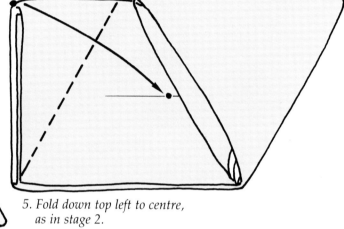

5. Fold down top left to centre, as in stage 2.

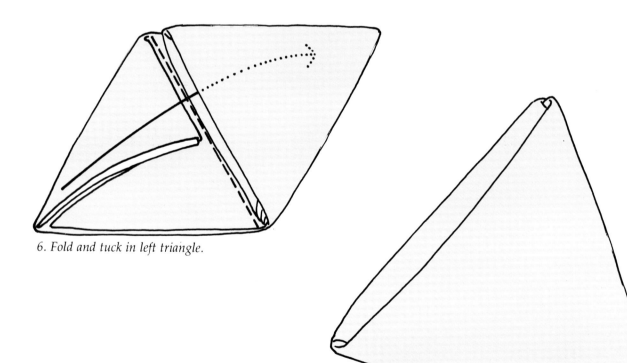

6. Fold and tuck in left triangle.

Fish

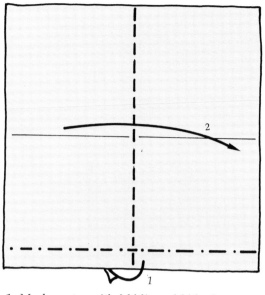

1. Mark centre with fold lines, fold back bottom edge approx. one-twelfth, then fold into two.

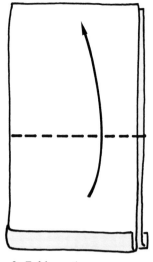

2. Fold up along centre line.

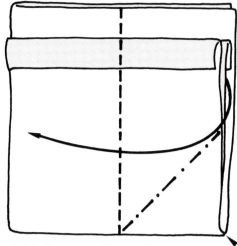

3. Mark centre with a fold and open up bottom right corner to form a triangle.

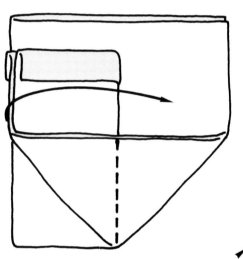

4. Take flap to right side.

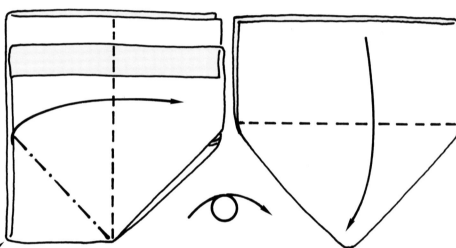

5. Open up bottom left corner and fold up as in stage 3. Turn back flap and turn over.

6. Fold down top two layers.

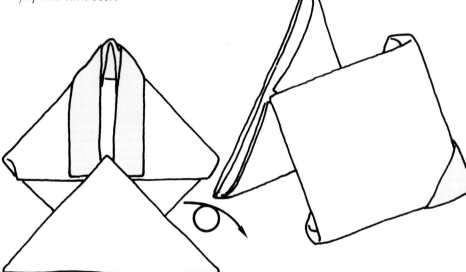

7. Fold down top corners to meet at centre and fold back the sides to form a triangle.

8. Turn over.

Book

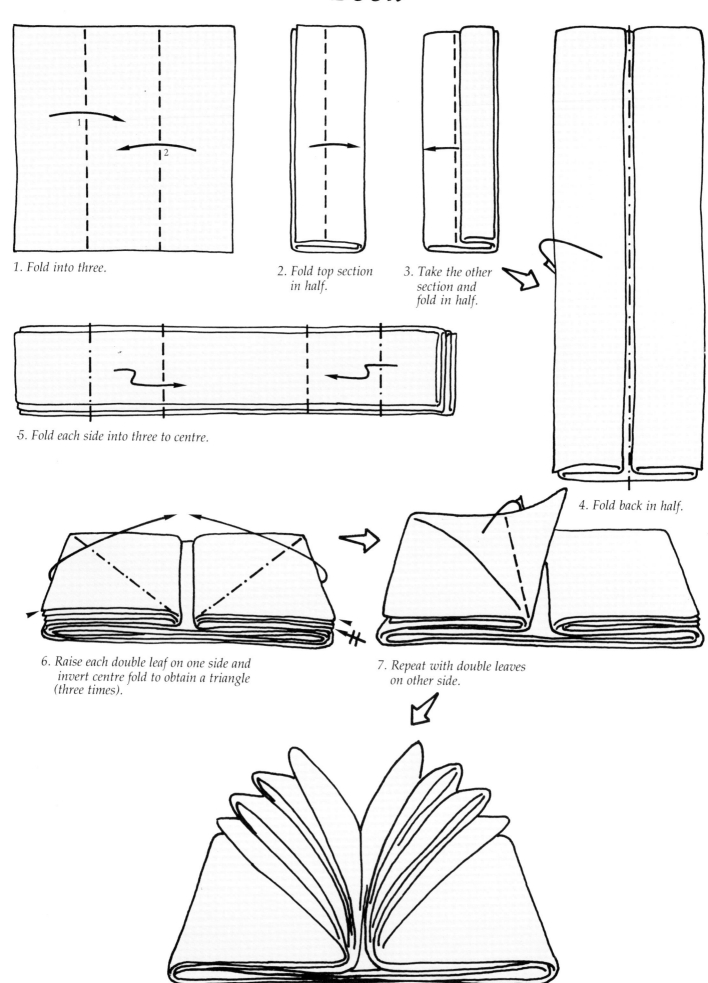

1. Fold into three.

2. Fold top section in half.

3. Take the other section and fold in half.

4. Fold back in half.

5. Fold each side into three to centre.

6. Raise each double leaf on one side and invert centre fold to obtain a triangle (three times).

7. Repeat with double leaves on other side.

Sun

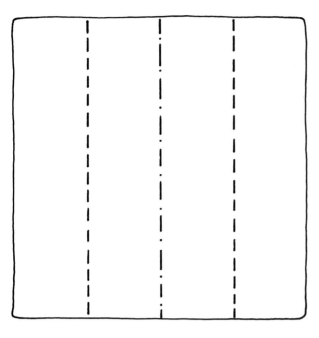

1. *Fold into four accordion pleats.*

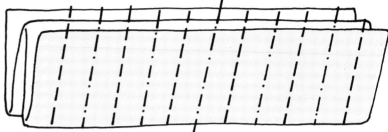

2. *Make eleven equal accordion pleats.*

3. *Tightly press all folds.*

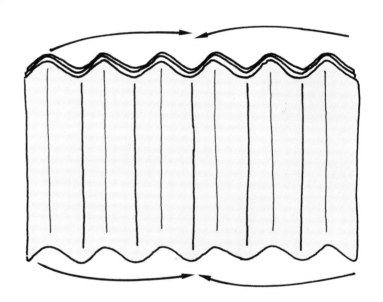

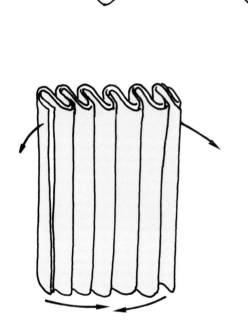

4. *Pinch base together and fan out.*

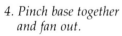

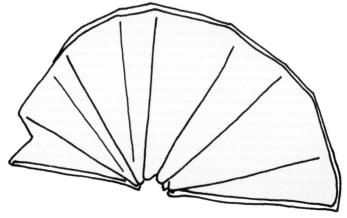

Flame

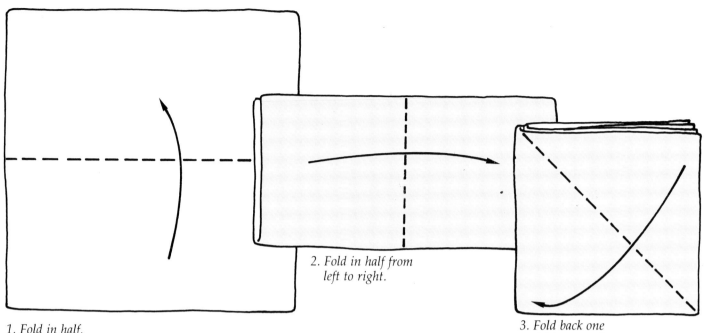

1. Fold in half.

2. Fold in half from left to right.

3. Fold back one thickness and turn.

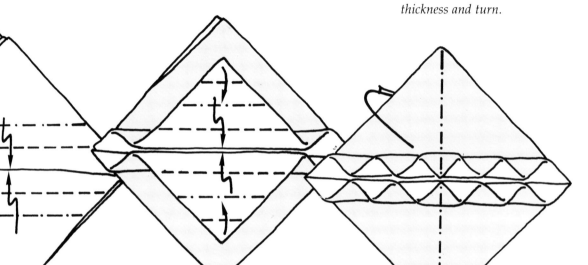

4. Take top and bottom layer and make three accordion pleats in each. Continue folding accordion style.

5. Fold back in half.

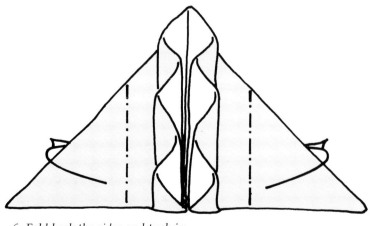

6. Fold back the sides and tuck in.

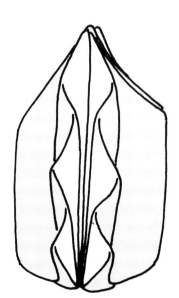

Fan

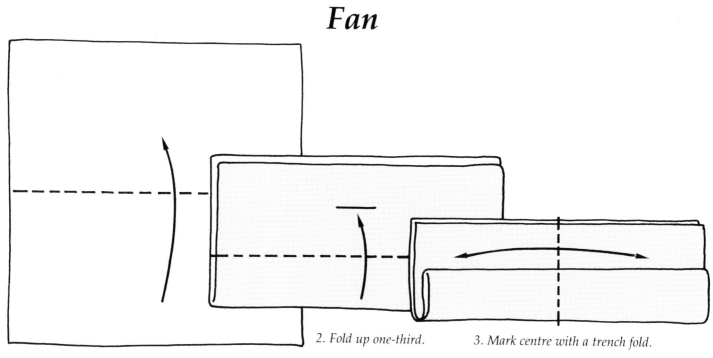

1. Fold into two.

2. Fold up one-third.

3. Mark centre with a trench fold.

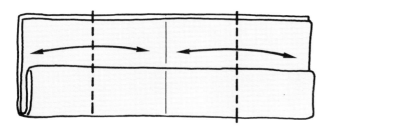

4. Similarly mark quarters.

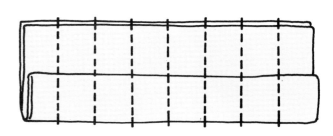

5. Mark the eighths.

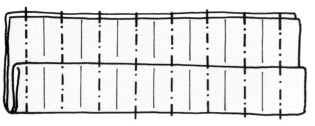

6. Make eight accordion pleats.

7b. Hold on to end, lift up triangles in each fold and open out.

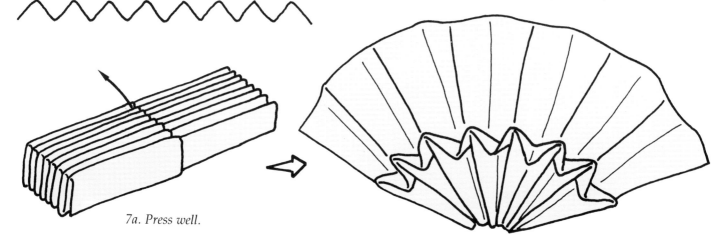

7a. Press well.

Fountain

1. Fold up into two.

2. Fold into two again.

3. Fold top down one-third.

4. Mark centre and quarters with trench folds.

5. Mark eighths with trench folds.

6. Now make eight accordion pleats.

7. Place bottom into a stemmed glass.

Flamenco

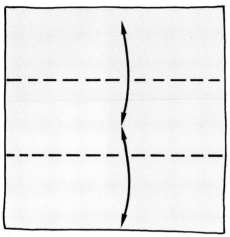

1. Mark the thirds.

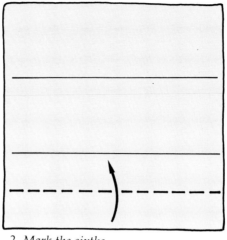

2. Mark the sixths.

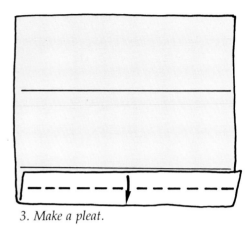

3. Make a pleat.

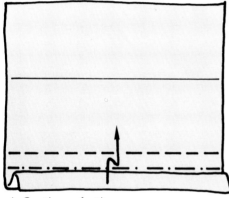

4. Continue pleating . . .

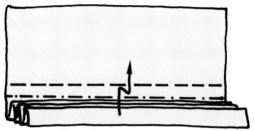

5. . . . until you have six accordion pleats.

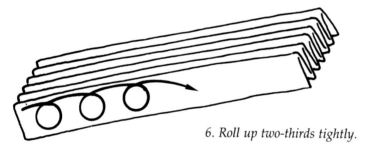

6. Roll up two-thirds tightly.

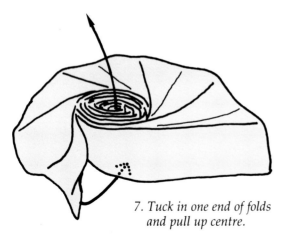

7. Tuck in one end of folds
and pull up centre.

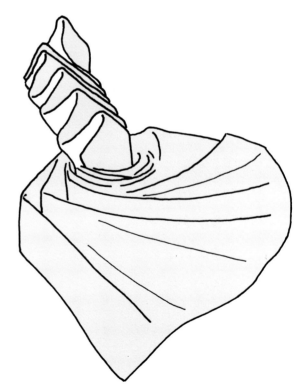

Dove

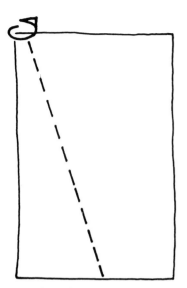

1. Take either a square or rectangular napkin and roll tightly at an angle.

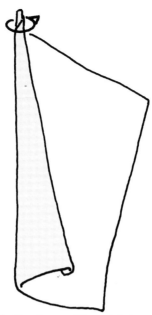

2. Continue rolling tightly pulling bottom at each turn.

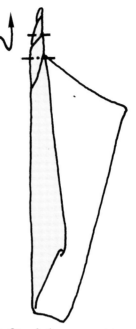

3. Stop before you get to end and make a pleat to form head.

4. Hold head and roll tightly to retain shape of beak and eyes . . .

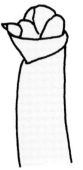

5. . . . like this.

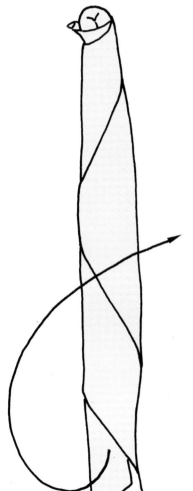

6. Roll to end and make a curl . . .

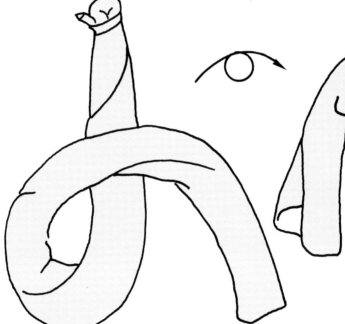

7. . . . like this. Turn over.

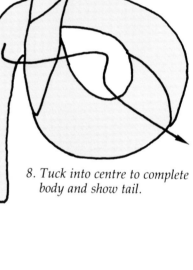

8. Tuck into centre to complete body and show tail.

Pleating

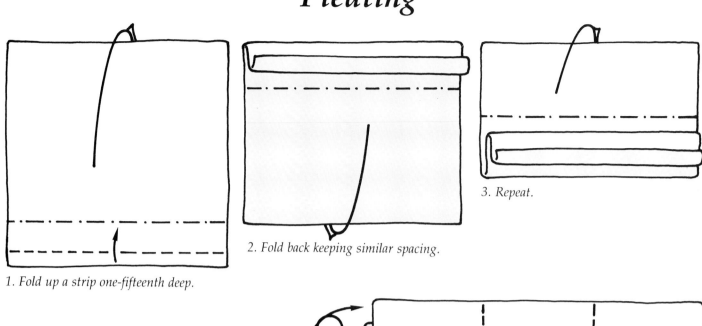

1. *Fold up a strip one-fifteenth deep.*

2. *Fold back keeping similar spacing.*

3. *Repeat.*

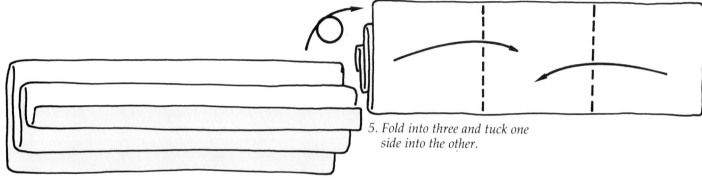

4. *It should look like this. Turn over.*

5. *Fold into three and tuck one side into the other.*

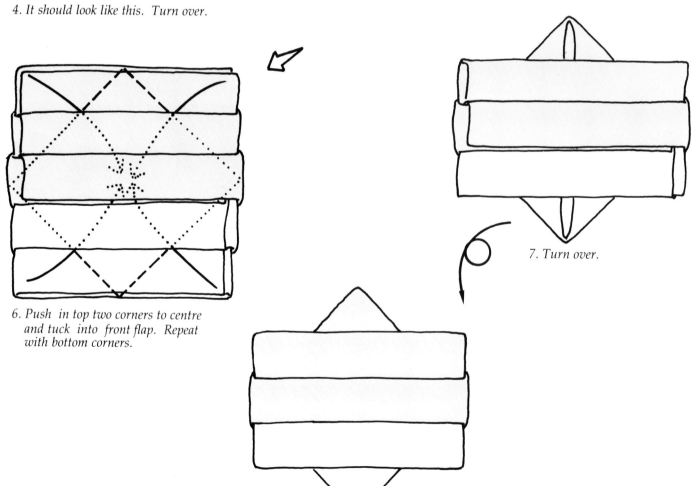

6. *Push in top two corners to centre and tuck into front flap. Repeat with bottom corners.*

7. *Turn over.*

Rose-bud

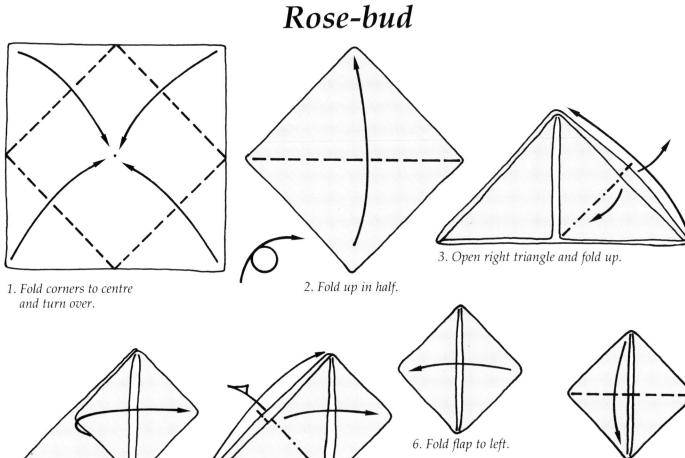

1. Fold corners to centre and turn over.

2. Fold up in half.

3. Open right triangle and fold up.

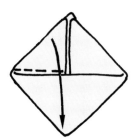

4. Fold flap to right.

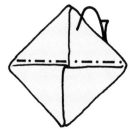

5. Repeat stage 3.

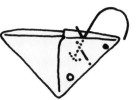

6. Fold flap to left.

7. Fold down top layer to base.

8. Fold down left triangle.

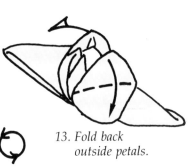

9. Fold top half to back.

10. Push right-hand corner inside.

11. Repeat with left-hand corner.

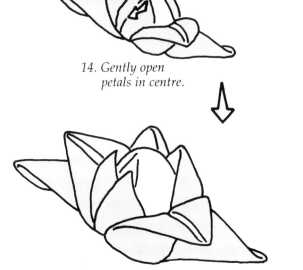

14. Gently open petals in centre.

12. Expand and turn upside-down.

13. Fold back outside petals.

Ear of corn

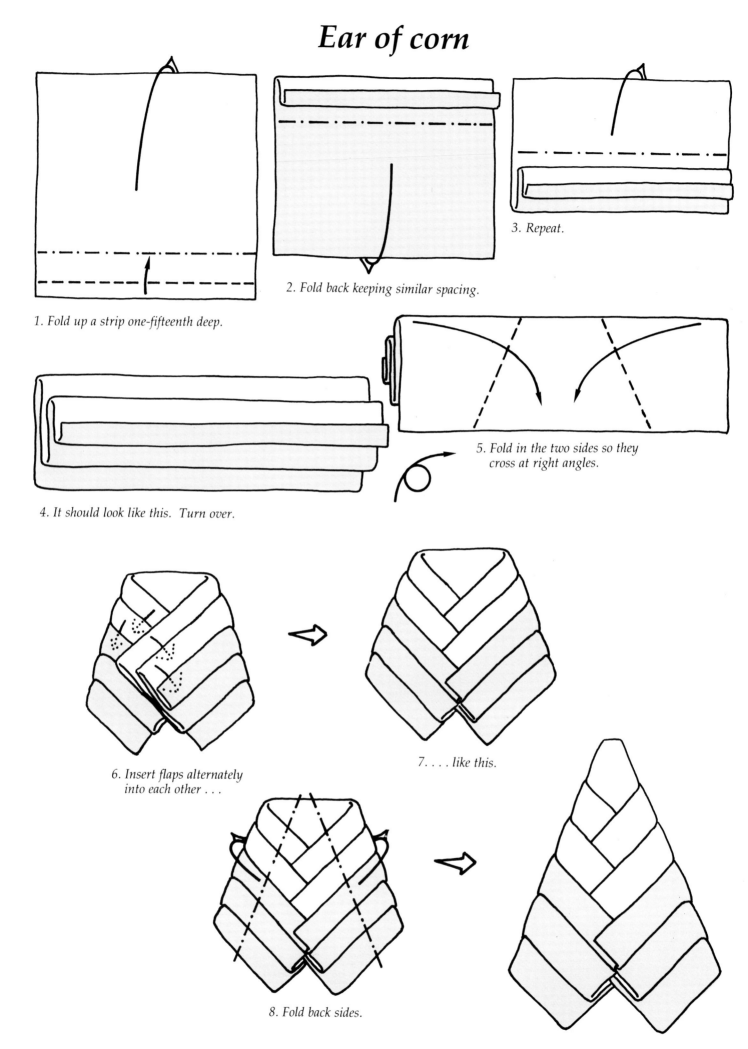

1. Fold up a strip one-fifteenth deep.

2. Fold back keeping similar spacing.

3. Repeat.

4. It should look like this. Turn over.

5. Fold in the two sides so they cross at right angles.

6. Insert flaps alternately into each other . . .

7. . . . like this.

8. Fold back sides.

Water-lily

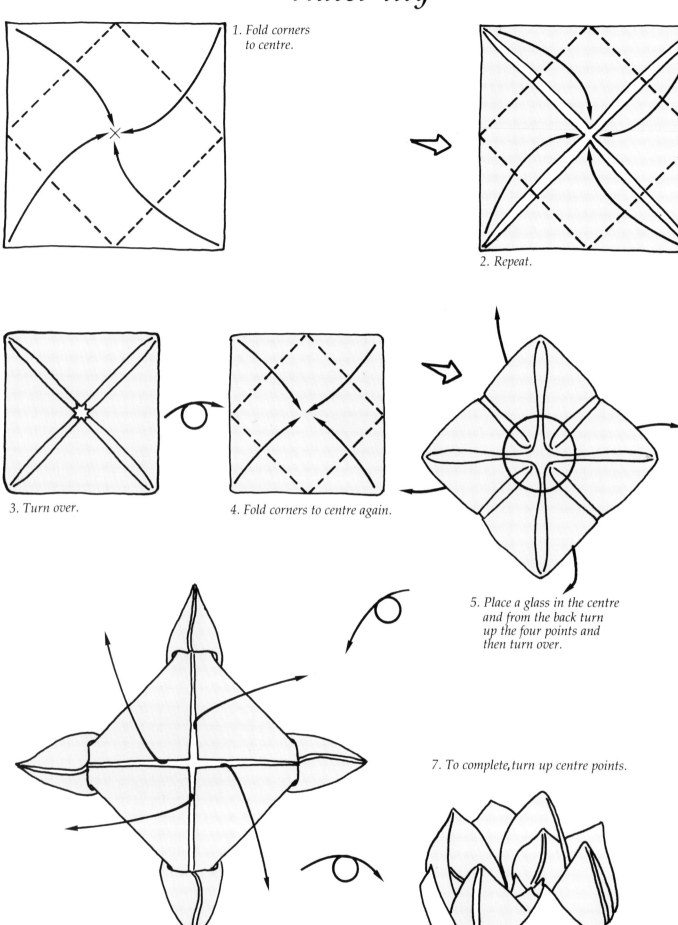

1. Fold corners to centre.

2. Repeat.

3. Turn over.

4. Fold corners to centre again.

5. Place a glass in the centre and from the back turn up the four points and then turn over.

6. Turn back the four corners and turn napkin over.

7. To complete, turn up centre points.

Orchid

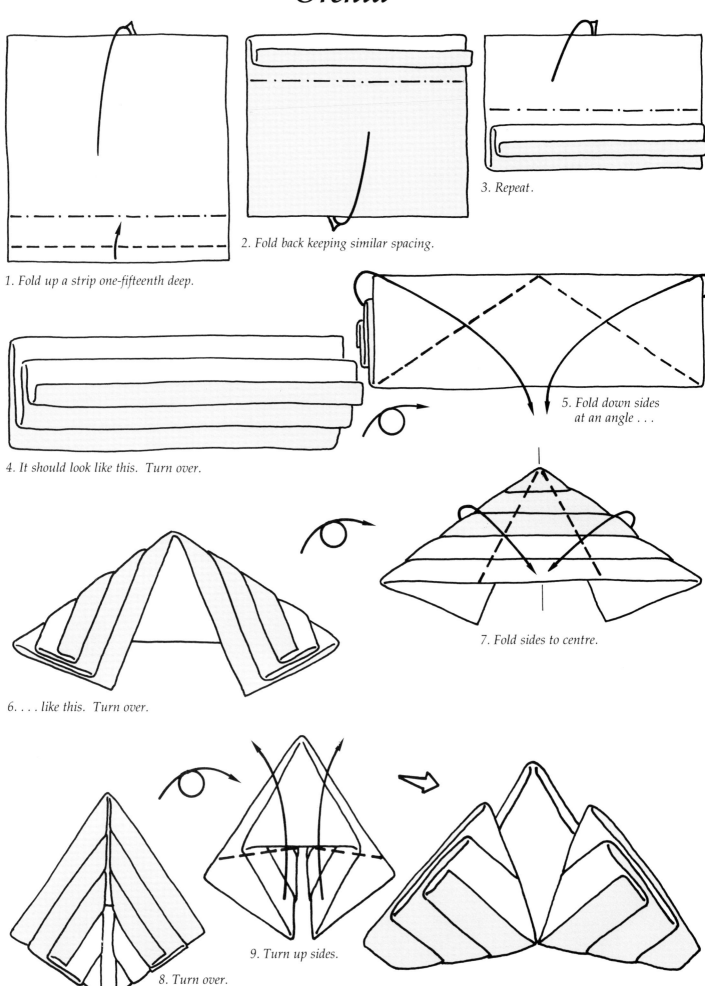

1. Fold up a strip one-fifteenth deep.

2. Fold back keeping similar spacing.

3. Repeat.

4. It should look like this. Turn over.

5. Fold down sides at an angle . . .

6. . . . like this. Turn over.

7. Fold sides to centre.

8. Turn over.

9. Turn up sides.

Shepherd

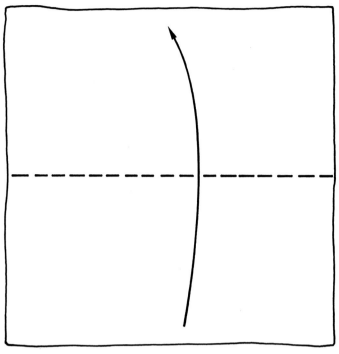

1. Fold into two.

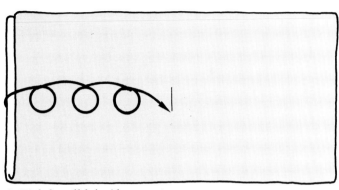

2. Tightly roll left side to centre.

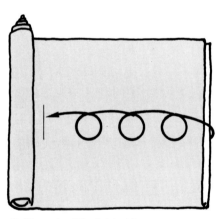

3. Repeat with right side . . .

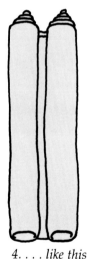

4. . . . like this.
Turn over.

5. Fold in half.

6. Turn right roll inside out like
a sock, take it forwards and
wrap round other three rolls.

7. Put in a spoon to
make a head.

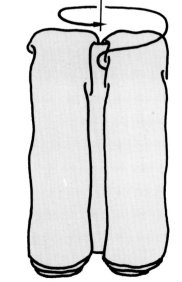

Butterfly

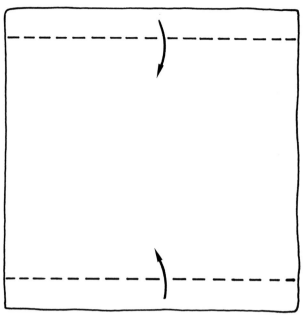

1. Fold over one-tenth at top and bottom.

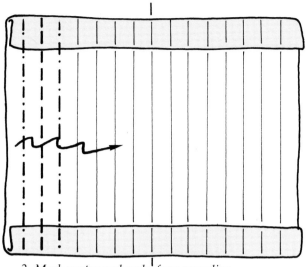

2. Mark centre and make four accordion pleats on each side.

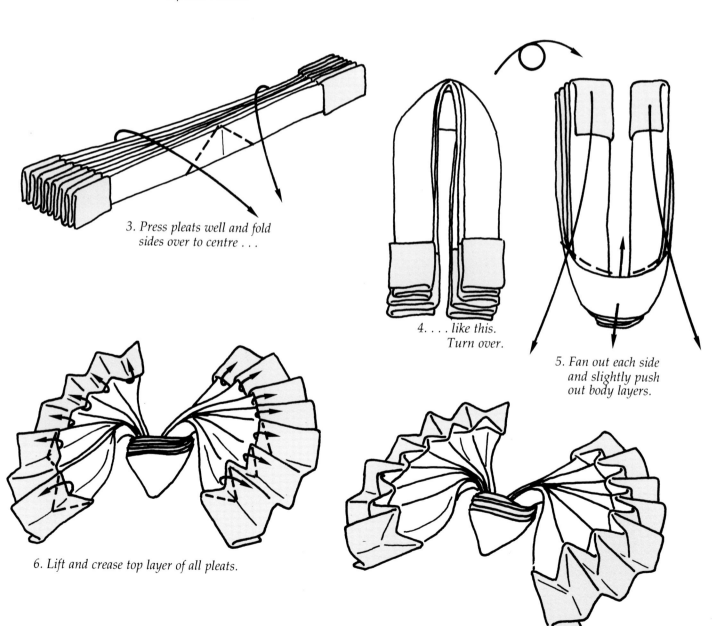

3. Press pleats well and fold sides over to centre . . .

4. . . . like this. Turn over.

5. Fan out each side and slightly push out body layers.

6. Lift and crease top layer of all pleats.

Hedgehog

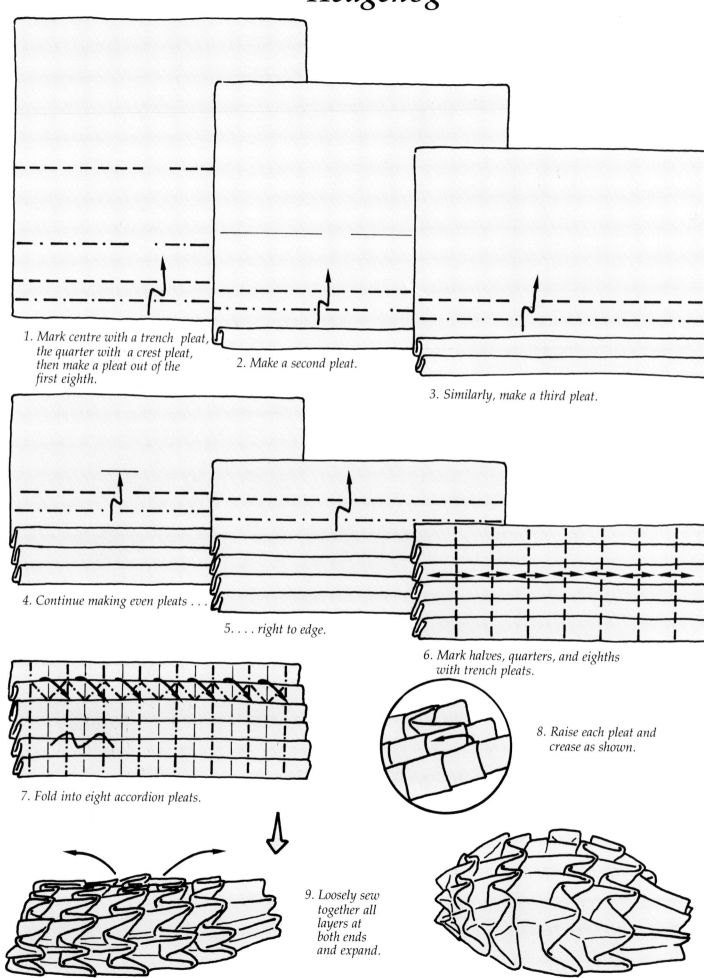

1. Mark centre with a trench pleat, the quarter with a crest pleat, then make a pleat out of the first eighth.

2. Make a second pleat.

3. Similarly, make a third pleat.

4. Continue making even pleats . . .

5. . . . right to edge.

6. Mark halves, quarters, and eighths with trench pleats.

7. Fold into eight accordion pleats.

8. Raise each pleat and crease as shown.

9. Loosely sew together all layers at both ends and expand.

Swan

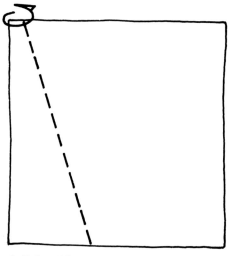

1. *Take either a square or rectangular napkin and roll tightly at an angle.*

2. *Continue rolling tightly, pulling bottom at each turn. Leave a section at end.*

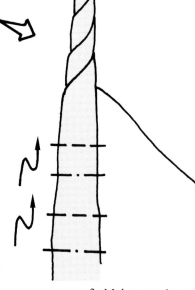

3. *Make two pleats as shown.*

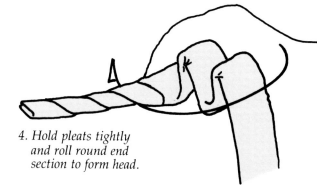

4. *Hold pleats tightly and roll round end section to form head.*

5. *Slide some wire inside to hold curve of neck.*

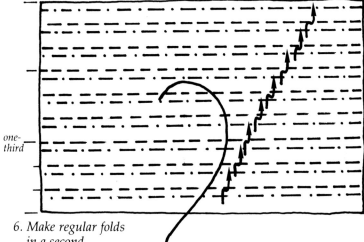

one-third

6. *Make regular folds in a second rectangular napkin.*

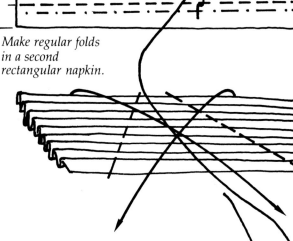

7. *Place head section on folded napkin and cross over. Bread rolls can be placed inside to give volume.*

Flat-fish

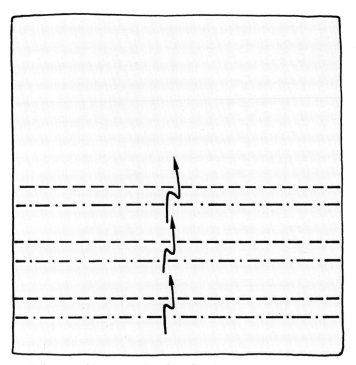

1. Take a napkin proportional to the size of fish you have in mind. As with the Hedgehog (see pages 90-1), make a series of regular folds to end.

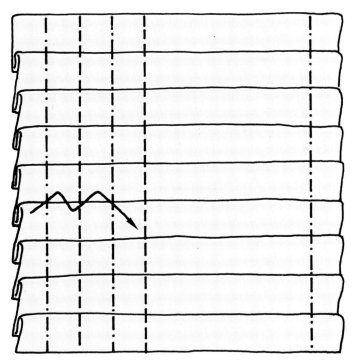

2. Make even accordion pleats across folds, the first and last should be a crest and you should have an even number of pleats . . .

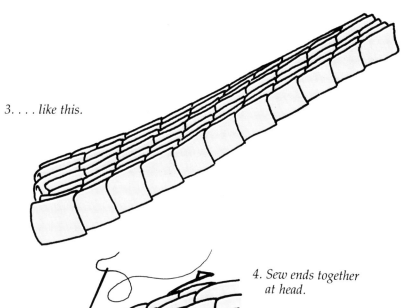

3. . . . like this.

5. To make tail, tie all folds with ribbon or sew together. Expand middle.

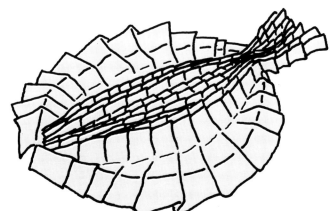

4. Sew ends together at head.

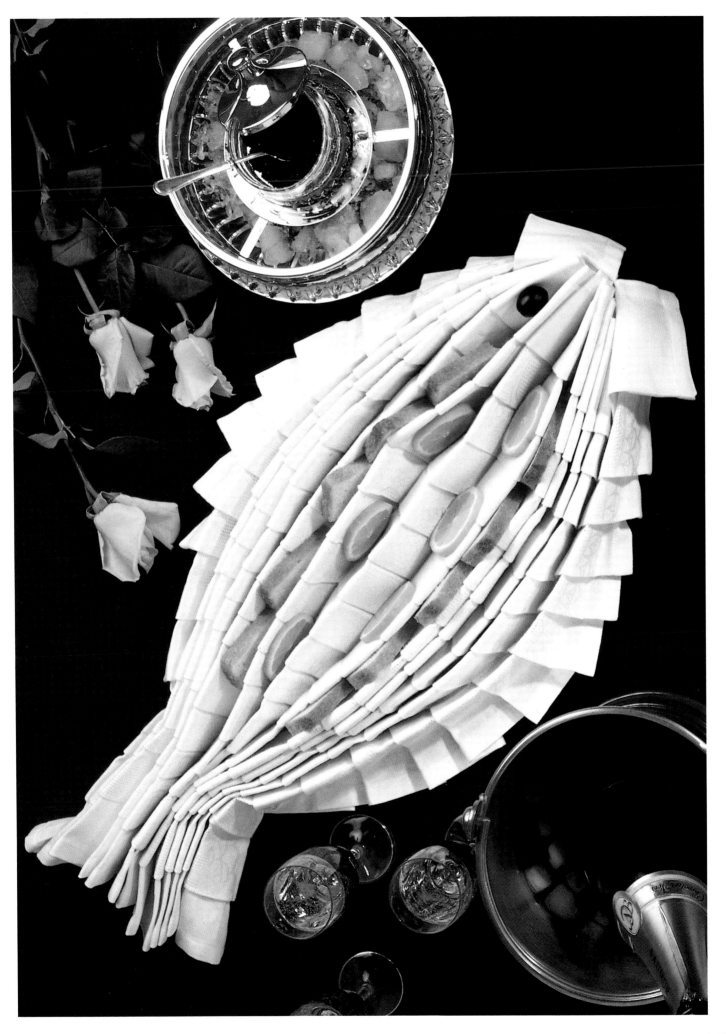

OTHER BOOKS PUBLISHED BY SEARCH PRESS

The Great Potato Cookbook
Jennifer Steel

The humble potato has potential few of us realize, and its amazing versatility is shown to mouth-watering effect in this book. There are over 100 recipes from forty countries to offer the housewife, working girl, or batchelor, a 'mix and mash' combination of starters, main courses, puddings, and wines.

Decorating Cakes for Children's Parties
Polly Pinder

Thirty-one cakes are 'tastefully' illustrated in full colour, with 424 step-by-step drawings to inspire the reader to make these stunning and delightful cakes. Ideas range from Humpty Dumpty and Superman to Winnie the Pooh and the Fast-food addict.

Creative Handmade Paper
David Watson

This book shows how to be creative and environmentally friendly using recycled papers and plant materials to make unusual textured papers. Using household equipment, David Watson shows the simple task of transforming old papers, plants, leaves, straw, and other organic materials into beautiful handmade paper.

Simple Decorative Paper Techniques
Stéphane Ipert and Florent Rousseau

This book shows how to transform plain papers into an amazing selection of decorative and colourful papers, using ingenious techniques with just a handful of simple equipment. There are easy instructions on how to spray, stipple, and stencil to produce an explosion of random colour designs; how to create swirls, stripes, squares, and other patterns using coloured pastes and a variety of simple tools; and, finally, how to produce stunning abstract patterns using inked rollers, resist techniques, and a special 'tie-dye' method.

Marbling on Paper
Using Oil Paints
Anne Chambers

In *Marbling on Paper*, Anne Chambers shows, in easy stages, how you can master this beautiful and decorative technique. Learn traditional and contemporary methods, including spattered or stone marbling, marble cut, patterned, combed, and stormont effects. There is also a brief history of this unique art, together with ideas for using marbled papers.

The Craft of Temari
Mary Wood

Described as 'embroidering the surface of a ball', this ancient Japanese craft shows how to use delicate stitching and wrapping techniques with an array of colourful threads to form individual and beautiful surface patterns.

Candlemaking
Creative Designs and Techniques
David Constable

Packed with ideas and step-by-step practical instructions, *Candlemaking* shows how to make a marvellous selection of dipped, moulded, and novelty candles. The candles illustrated range from simple twisted, one-colour, and perfumed candles, to exotic snakes, multicoloured landscapes, and dramatic water candles. There is also a wealth of ideas for finishing and embellishing the surface of the candles.

Illuminated Alphabets
Patricia Carter

In her usual delicate and original style, Patricia Carter has created nine complete alphabets which will inspire artists, calligraphers, and embroiderers alike to design and decorate capital letters. Her beautiful alphabet designs include Simple leaf, Entwined roses, Parchment, Classical collection, Ribbons, and Harlequin, each of which is illustrated in colour with full instructions on the basic design, plus ideas for variations.

Painted Eggs
Heidi Haupt-Battaglia

There are many ideas and instructions for painting and dyeing eggs: using natural and chemical dyes with engraving; painting flowers and landscapes in watercolours and gouache; drawing with pencils, felt-tipped pens, inks, and chalk; and using batik and stencilling methods.

A Complete Guide to Silk Painting
Susanne Hahn

This definitive guide to silk painting is a unique treasury of ideas, designs, and techniques that follows the 'Silk Road' of discovery from fibre through to fabric, and takes you step by step through the different techniques of this fascinating art. Inside, you will find beautiful colour illustrations detailing the history of the silk trade in Asia and Europe, and the development of the modern silk-making process. There is also information and advice on materials and equipment, and many ideas for gift and home-furnishing projects.

Drawing for Pleasure
Edited by Valerie C. Douet

This new, revised edition of *Drawing for Pleasure* contains examples of the work of fourteen artists, in a wide range of media that includes pencil, charcoal, Conté, felt-tipped pen, crayon, and wash. A valuable reference work for anyone learning to draw, it gives sound, practical instruction on line, tone, perspective, and composition. It also demonstrates to the more experienced student how to capture the mood of a subject by subtle methods, which can only be imparted by experts who are also teachers.

If you are interested in any of the above books, or any of the art and craft titles published by Search Press, then please send for a free catalogue to:

SEARCH PRESS LTD.,
Dept. B, Wellwood, North Farm Road, Tunbridge Wells, Kent TN2 3DR